A true story from the Bible

This is the story of how God sent someone

to fix everything.

That someone
         was called Jesus.

They closed their eyes.
They closed their hearts.
They said no to God.

When Jesus' friends came back,
the big stone door was open!
"Jesus is ...

not here!"

"He's alive! He's all better!" blinding-bright angels told them.

"Don't you remember? Jesus told you he had to die and come back alive again!"

It wasn't Jesus who said no to God.
It wasn't Jesus who wasn't kind.
It wasn't Jesus who should be
put on a cross.

But

Jesus died

for

us.

Jesus didn't come just to fix a few things.

He gave his life to fix the thing
that makes everything broken ...

our broken friendship with God.

Now anyone
who believes in Jesus

is friends with God.

He came alive again,
 to show us how one day, in heaven,
  EVERYTHING will be fixed
   for God's friends,
    for ever.

Notes for grown-ups

This story comes from Luke 24 v 1-8, but it starts right back at the beginning of the Bible. Here it tells us that God made a perfect world but that people disobeyed his rules—they said no to God. They were not friends with God anymore, and because of this, the whole world became broken. Sadness, hatred, illness and death came into our lives; we cannot live for ever anymore. Our broken friendship with God is *"the thing that makes everything broken"*. But someone was coming to fix it!

The Bible tells us that God came into the world as a person, Jesus Christ, with no guilt of his own to pay for. Jesus paid the punishment for when *we* have said no to God and his rules—the punishment of death, the most broken of brokenness. Now, if we believe in Jesus, we can be friends with God. But Jesus did not stay dead: *"He is not here,"* said the angels by his grave (v 6, NIV). He came alive again, the first person ever to do so. He is like the first fruits on a tree, showing us that the punishment of death was paid, and that God will bring his friends back to life for ever too, in a world that is all fixed.

Some people did not love God, and still said no, closing their hearts to the one God sent. But Jesus welcomes everyone who comes to him and says yes to God. Because of Jesus, we can be friends with God for ever.

Luke 24 v 1-8
(The Bible: New International Version)

[1] On the first day of the week, very early in the morning, the women took the spices they had prepared and went to the tomb. [2] They found the stone rolled away from the tomb, [3] but when they entered, they did not find the body of the Lord Jesus.

[4] While they were wondering about this, suddenly two men in clothes that gleamed like lightning stood beside them. [5] In their fright the women bowed down with their faces to the ground, but the men said to them, "Why do you look for the living among the dead? [6] He is not here; he has risen! Remember how he told you, while he was still with you in Galilee: [7] 'The Son of Man must be delivered over to the hands of sinners, be crucified and on the third day be raised again.'" [8] Then they remembered his words.

Little me
BIG GOD

Collect the series

- The Man Who Would Not Be Quiet • Never Too Little • The Best Thing To Do
- The Dad Who Never Gave Up • The Boy Who Shared His Sandwich
- The Easter Fix • The Little Man Whose Heart Grew Big
- How Can I Pray? • The House That Went Splat • The Christmas Surprise

The Easter Fix
© Stephanie Williams, 2021.
Reprinted 2021, 2023.

Published by:
The Good Book Company

thegoodbook.com | thegoodbook.co.uk
thegoodbook.com.au | thegoodbook.co.nz | thegoodbook.co.in

Unless indicated, all Scripture references are taken from the Holy Bible, New International Version. Copyright © 2011 Biblica. Used by permission.

Stephanie Williams has asserted her right under the Copyright, Designs and Patents Act 1988 to be identified as the author and illustrator of this work.

All rights reserved. Except as may be permitted by the Copyright Act, no part of this publication may be reproduced in any form or by any means without prior permission from the publisher.

ISBN: 9781784985844 | JOB-007509 | Printed in India